PROTECTING CITIES FROM WILDFIRES

Protecting Cities From Wildfires
Improving California's Land-Use, Water And Brush-Clearance Strategies
Volume Eight

Steven Greenhut

August 2025

ISBN: 978-1-934276-59-4

Pacific Research Institute
P.O. Box 60485
Pasadena, CA 91116

www.pacificresearch.org

PROTECTING CITIES FROM WILDFIRES
IMPROVING CALIFORNIA'S LAND-USE, WATER AND BRUSH-CLEARANCE STRATEGIES

By Steven Greenhut

VOLUME EIGHT

PR∥ PACIFIC
RESEARCH
INSTITUTE

Introduction: Wildfires Should Serve As Wake-Up Call

News reports cite the beginning of the 2025 Los Angeles fires on January 7 at 10:30 am, as the Santa Ana winds blew a cloud of black smoke over heavily populated areas in and around Los Angeles. An hour or so later, NBC 4 Los Angeles reported[1] that "gridlock formed on Sunset Boulevard," which "blocked people in traffic for miles as they desperately tried to evacuate and get away from the dangerous flames. The Palisades Fire quickly expanded, consuming homes, cars and anything in its path." The Eaton Fire in the San Gabriel Mountains began that evening.

The nightmarish situation grew worse rather quickly. The two fires (and five smaller ones) ultimately consumed more than 37,000 acres. When it was all over 24 days later, the fires claimed 30 lives and more than 16,000 homes and other structures, and caused the evacuations of 180,000 people.[2] Insurance companies expect losses of more than $30 billion, with total economic damage pegged at more than $250 billion.[3] They were not only among the most destructive wildfires ever in California, but among the costliest natural disasters in U.S. history.

California, of course, has experienced wildfires since time immemorial. And only seven years ago, the Camp Fire in the northeastern county of Butte burned 153,000 acres, claimed 85 lives and destroyed the small down of Paradise, not far from the college town of Chico.[4] It didn't cause as much economic damage as the latest fires, but it was bigger and even deadlier. In its short history of California wildfires, the Western Fire Chiefs Association (WFCA) noted that the state's first recorded wildfire was in 1889. It burned 300,000 acres in Orange, San Diego and Riverside counties after Santa Ana winds descended on the drought-parched region. Official state wildfire records didn't begin until 1932, but the list of major, destructive fires is exceedingly long.[5]

Yet despite all the evidence that California—thanks to its frequent droughts, Santa Ana winds and warm temperatures—has always been home to such weather events, the WFCA repeats the standard explanation promoted by California officials. "Some of California's largest, deadliest and most destructive wildfires have occurred within the last five years," it explained. "This is due to climate change which is a result of humans burning fossil fuels which create greenhouse gases that warm up our planet. Global warming causes both land and air to become drier than normal, thus making the perfect conditions for wildfires to ignite."[6]

That may be so (and it is beyond the purview of this booklet to debate manmade climate change), but it's also possible the state has seen some of the deadliest and most destructive fires in modern times rather than a century ago because of the size of our population and value of the built environment. It's obvious, but worth repeating: California's population in 1889 was 1.2 million. It was 5.9 million in 1932. It's 39 million today.[7] The state also has changed the way it battles wildfires in recent decades. I don't doubt that the climate is warming or that fires have gotten particularly severe since 2018, but I fear that California's climate-change approach is a case where ideology and misplaced priorities make the state more vulnerable to wildfires.

Specifically, state officials have embraced policies—an attempted ban on internal-combustion vehicles, a cap-and-trade system designed to reduce industrial carbon emissions, etc.—that are designed to change the trajectory of the Earth's climate. California accounts for less than 1% of global greenhouse emissions, so the apparent and often-stated goal of state officials is to prod the rest of the country to embrace similar policies.[8] Otherwise, our progress won't make any difference. It's always seemed bizarre that a state government that can't even, say, manage its own budget and infrastructure effectively thinks that it can somehow make a dent in a problem of such scientific complexity and that involves 195 international governments.

Instead of taking this overly ambitious approach, it seems wiser for the state government to embrace policies that improve our *resilience* to changing weather patterns. That's the focus of this booklet: How California can improve its wildfire-fighting approach, rejigger its insurance policies, bolster its water resources and streamline its building processes.

A 2022 University of Chicago study found that a "single year of wildfire emissions is close to double emissions reductions achieved over 16 years."[9] Our state leaders are obsessed with reducing pollution, yet the study found "the wildfires lead to pollution that is set to shave nearly a year off the life expectancy of residents in California's most polluted counties if pollution levels persist." Wildfires in 2020 made up 30% of the state's greenhouse gases.

Perhaps a more attainable agenda is in order. And there is much to attain. I argued the following in my testimony to the U.S. House Judiciary Committee's subcommittee evaluating the impact of California regulations on the state's recent wildfires:[10]

> The Los Angeles wildfires … have exposed festering regulatory hurdles that have exacerbated the crisis. Many are years in the making, maddeningly complex and not given to quick solutions. It's a confluence of bad policy involving brush clearance, water, insurance, firefighting, housing and climate change. Simply put, California has created a tangled web of regulation that renders this once-innovative state incapable of accomplishing anything efficiently.

In other words, there are plenty of policies California can embrace to reduce wildfires and their impact on our society, but it has to get its priorities in order. California has thousands of wildfires every year, but seeing one claim large sections of the nation's second-largest city and its environs certainly puts the 2025 fires in a different perspective. It reminded everyone that wildfires—and the state and local response to them—also are a major urban issue.

As Headwaters Economics explained:[11]

> The fires in Los Angeles follow a pattern starting to become familiar. As was seen in Hawaii's Lahaina Fire, Colorado's Marshall Fire and Oregon's Almeda Fire, wind-driven embers from nearby wildfires ignited homes, which spread fire rapidly to neighboring homes, becoming an urban conflagration. Also known as urban wildfires, these large, difficult-to-control fires may start as wildfires but, upon entering communities, buildings become the source of fuel. It is the building-to-building transmission that causes widespread destruction that can occur in communities of any size.

While I don't put much stock in the chiefs' association's assessment of global climate, it is right on point as it discusses the increasing effect of wildfires on urban communities. The fire threat has increased, it explains, as cities spread into the so-called Wildland Urban Interface—the wonky term for the heavily wooded outskirts. It calls for improved building codes that bolster the use of materials that resist fires. This booklet looks at some of those techniques later, focusing on "fire-wise" communities within high-risk areas that have avoided major fire problems thanks to this approach. The chiefs also argue that "using technology can allow for an approach to fire service that is more data-driven, proactive and faster. Data gathered from smart technology can provide insight on high-risk areas for fires, which helps in fire prevention and planning efforts."[12] That's less grandiose than banning fossil fuels—but it's more likely to yield productive and attainable results.

The increasing urban threat, of course, has sparked all the usual debates that dominate urban policy, including issues involving land use, density, climate change and transportation. Predictably, many voices on the Left and Right have used the fires to promote their hobby horses. For instance, some claim that higher densities boost fire risk because fires can more easily spread among attached housing, whereas others claim that low-density housing is a higher risk as many single-family homes are nestled among trees and other brush. Not surprisingly, those arguments always reinforce each side's previously existing preference for either high- or low-density living.

California YIMBY (Yes In My Back Yard) argues that,[13] "Policies that promote higher-density, clustered development within existing urban areas can substantially reduce the future risk of housing loss due to wildfires." The group admits that "this approach aligns with broader ecological and conservation goals, highlighting the importance of strategic planning in mitigating wildfire impacts." The group's point is that clustered development reduces construction in that wildlands interface area.

Meanwhile, Randal O'Toole (a former Cato Institute land-use writer whose articles occasionally appear on the Free Cities Center web page) argues that the Los Angeles tragedy "is a direct result of so-called 'smart-growth' policies that call for establishing greenbelts around cities and packing people in high-density housing within those cities."[14] His point is that fires spread more rapidly when houses are attached or close to one another, especially when surrounded by government-mandated open space.

I see the value in every type of neighborhood, with higher densities serving the preferences of some people and lower densities serving the desires of others. The issue deserves serious study, but I'm opposed to the government using its various tools such as zoning or other regulations to mandate one type or another. This booklet opposes using the wildfire threat as a means to champion one land-use preference over another. In keeping with the Free Cities Center's mission of promoting freer markets and more consumer choice, it explores how government policies can reduce wildfire risk for every type of urban community—so Californians don't have to relive the nightmare in Pacific Palisades and Altadena, the San Gabriel Valley community that was largely reduced to ashes.[15]

We shouldn't be myopic. Part of life in California, especially Southern California, involves accepting the ever-present threats of natural disaster. Just as Iowans must always deal with tornadoes and Floridians must always brace for hurricanes, Californians must always prepare for fire and wind. As the noted California author Joan Didion wrote in 1968, "Los Angeles weather handing out the permits, claims[31] that removing the plants would increase fire risk. Whatever the reality, this much-delayed six-year-old upgrade project highlights the multiple agencies, lawsuits and disputes that delay progress, increase costs and leave California communities vulnerable to the wiles of nature.

The various L.A. screw-ups were sufficiently publicized to push Gov. Gavin Newsom to order investigations. "I am calling for an independent investigation into the loss of water pressure to local fire hydrants and the reported unavailability of water supplies from the Santa Ynez Reservoir," the governor wrote in a post on X. "We need answers to ensure this does not happen again and we have every resource available to fight these catastrophic fires."[32] That's fine enough, although the state has a habit of investigating governmental miscues—then doing little to implement the ultimate findings.

It's time for officials to get busy fixing the underlying policy impediments—so then it won't need to spend as much time pondering what went wrong.

is the weather of catastrophe, of apocalypse, and, just as the reliably long and bitter winters of New England determine the way life is lived there, so the violence and the unpredictability of the Santa Ana affect the entire quality of life in Los Angeles, accentuate its impermanence, its unreliability."[16] Still, there's much that California and its officials can do to minimize any potential apocalypse.

Sadly, it took a tragic event to expose many of the failed policies currently embraced by state and local governments. This booklet looks at California's failed brush-clearance, water, insurance and housing policies—the latter of particular importance as Los Angeles begins the rebuilding process. It proposes fixes that are simple in concept (although certainly not in implementation). In most cases, they involve reducing the California government's heavy hand of regulation, thus allowing property owners, insurers and developers to create safer and more fire-resistant communities.

Putting the Spotlight on Governmental Incompetence

Following the Los Angeles wildfires, Angelenos understandably took a negative view of the city's leadership, per the 10th annual UCLA/Luskin School Quality of Life Index published in April 2024: "Mayor Karen Bass has seen her popularity flip to a negative standing throughout the county. The net 20-point overall decline in her favorability rating was matched by her fall among Latinos, doubled in the white community (a stunning 40-point turnaround), far outpacing the more minor decline among Asian/Pacific Islanders and the actual slight improvement for Bass among African American county residents."[17] Her overall favorability ratings were a dismal 37%.

The wildfires imprinted horrific images on the public psyche, ranging from photos of the charred remains of historic buildings, residents stuck in traffic as they tried to escape the cascading hellscape, people mourning their lost loved ones and massive blazes careening over hillsides. But few Californians will forget perhaps the worst political image of the fires. Right before the wildfires hit, Bass had flown to Ghana to attend the inauguration of the country's president. As she arrived home in Los Angeles, a reporter from Sky News, David Blevins, questioned her outside the plane.[18]

"No, I'm not going to do that," Bass said. "Have you absolutely nothing to say to the citizens today who are dealing with this disaster?" Blevins asked. She stared silently and awkwardly in response for nearly two minutes. Bass had been widely criticized for leaving on the journey despite news reports about the intensifying fire risk. In an interview with the local Fox affiliate, she addressed the encounter: "Yes, it was an ambush. And I wasn't sure who that was. It is unfortunate because I see how that looks as if I was avoiding but when you're getting off a plane you've been on for 17 hours and someone hits you with a camera...I wish...in hindsight...my response had been better."[19]

That's fair enough, but didn't soften the blowback. One disastrously bad interview doesn't necessarily end a politician's career, but her deer-in-the-headlights response reinforced the perception that city officials hadn't effectively responded to the disaster. In February, Bass dismissed Fire Chief Kristin Crowley for inadequately preparing for the devastation—raising questions that she used the chief as a scapegoat. "The mayor said the former chief had failed to deploy 1,000 off-duty firefighters," CBS News reported.[20] "However, a city ordinance states that in emergency preparedness and response, the mayor's office is the director who issues and enforces 'rules, regulations, orders,' including the deployment of additional personnel." The chief said the city had failed her department.

She's pointed to her December 2023 memo to the city, which warned that "budgetary reductions have adversely affected the Department's ability to maintain core operations, such as technology and communication infrastructure, payroll processing, training, fire prevention, and community education."[21] Others have disputed that allegation. "Jack Humphreville, who serves on the watchdog group Neighborhood Council Budget Advocates, said the fire department had to scale back operations to make way for employee raises," according to a *Los Angeles Times* report.[22] The report noted that the department, under Crowley's leadership, overspent its budget on overtime pay. But the dispute highlighted the city's inability to stay on top of its firefighting operations.

The issues went much deeper than the miscues of elected and appointed officials. Many of the high-profile failures also exposed deeper policy problems, which focus heavily on misplaced budget priorities and bureaucratic delays. As the *Los Angeles Times* reported, the city in 1961 had a reckoning over wildfire infrastructure after a fire destroyed 500 homes in Bel-Air and Brentwood. As a result, officials "built a reservoir in Santa Ynez Canyon, as well as a pumping station 'to increase fire protection,' as the L.A. Department of Water and Power's then-chief water engineer, Gerald W. Jones, told the *Times* in 1972."[23]

So where was the Santa Ynez reservoir in 2025? Sitting empty, as the Los Angeles Department of Water and Power and the state Water Resources Control Board tussled over repairs to a tear in the cover used to limit the accumulation of debris, as required by federal regulations. Ultimately, the newspaper reported, the state forced local officials to empty the reservoir to make the repairs—even though it had sat coverless with no appreciable problem as late as 2012.[24] "Former and current DWP officials acknowledge that if the reservoir had held water, higher-elevation areas of the Palisades would have had more water pressure, but it's unclear for how long," per the newspaper.

Speaking of water pressure, a KCAL News investigation[25] found that 1,300 hydrants throughout the city needed repair—with some in the wildfire area having been out of service for more than a year. Firefighters complained about a loss of pressure. That's understandable to some degree given that the hydrant system isn't designed to handle the demand placed by such a massive fire. However, another *Times* article found that "the limitations raise several questions: As fires grow larger and more intense in the West, should storage tanks and other local water infrastructure be expanded to contend with them? Where? And at what cost?"[26]

Since wildfires are such a common and growing problem, why hasn't the city upgraded the system or at least had this discussion? Part of the answer is tied to budget priorities. Writing in *City Journal*, the Manhattan Institute's Steven Malanga looked at the current mayor's own financial decisions:[27]

> Mayor Karen Bass's budget cuts to the city's fire department, enacted just months ago amid warnings about the city's deteriorating finances, stand out as a striking example of misplaced priorities. The cuts stemmed from a budget crisis triggered by her administration's decision to reward city employees with rich contracts and benefits—even as it dismissed worries that the reductions would hurt services.

This isn't just a blame game. I've extensively reported on California's budget priorities and the way local governments focus heavily on rewarding politically powerful unions at the expense of bolstering nuts-and-bolts city services. Municipal officials, especially in liberal big cities such as Los Angeles, complain about limited revenues, but that doesn't stop them from continually ratcheting up the compensation packages for workers. Crowley earned a total compensation package of nearly $655,000. Multiple Los Angeles fire officials earned total pay packages in the $600,000 to $900,000 range.[28]

Obviously, if the city offers such generous pay scales it limits the amount of money it has to hire additional firefighters and make other firefighting investments. Like many California cities, Los Angeles is facing another pension crisis, as the costs for retired employees (especially firefighters and police) consume larger portions of the budget and force cutbacks in the number of current employees. In 2018, Scott Beyer (who penned a previous Free Cities Center booklet) explained that "between 2003 and 2012, pension costs grew by 25% annually, far outpacing the annual spending growth for core services."[29] Overly generous pensions for firefighters reduce the amount of overall firefighting services, too. These are the fruits of past budget decisions.

Then there are the bizarre examples of municipal miscues that point less toward officials' particular decision-making and more toward the common-sense-defying administrative rules and bureaucratic process that hamper even the least-controversial projects. Wildfires often are sparked by utility poles. Undergrounding the poles is one option, although it's quite costly and doesn't work in every situation. Another reasonable option is to replace wood poles with steel ones. Such a process was taking place throughout Pacific Palisades.

"In 2019, the LA Department of Water and Power (LADWP) began replacing nearly 100-year-old power line poles cutting through Topanga State Park, when the project was halted within days by conservationists outraged that federally endangered Braunton's milkvetch plants had been trampled during the process," the *New York Post* reported.[30] In a follow-up report in *Newsweek*, the California Coastal Commission, responsible for

Rethinking How California Addresses Brush Clearing

As always, the main issue confronting all of California's myriad crises—housing, homelessness, infrastructure, drought, budget and wildfires—is politics. The state's 2025-2026 budget,[33] is an astounding $322 billion. It's not only the largest state budget by far, but it's toward the top nationwide in per-capita spending. Whereas California was once known for having the nation's finest infrastructure and public services, it now routinely ranks on the bottom of lists looking at traffic congestion and public schools. Increasingly, the state's Democratic leadership prioritizes social-spending over basic infrastructure issues. And often the state doesn't maintain what it already has, as was made clear by the crumbling spillways at Oroville Dam in 2017 during a flood crisis. Legislative leaders applaud new earmarks, but seem less interested in evaluating whether the new spending actually fixes any given problem.

The state doesn't hide its arguably misshapen priorities. This is from the state's official 2023-2024 budget document:[34]

California is on the frontline of the global climate crisis with record-breaking heat, extreme flooding and devastating wildfires impacting communities across the state. The summer months of 2022 included extreme heat waves and drought conditions, and 2023 began with statewide flood events in the winter and spring. The 2021 and 2022 Budget Acts allocated approximately $54 billion over five years and delivered a climate agenda to fully integrate climate solutions with equity and economic opportunity. With critical investments in health, education and jobs the state's climate agenda is simultaneously confronting the crisis while building a more resilient, just and equitable future for all Californians.

These priorities often take an inexplicable form. The governor and Legislature spend their political capital blaming corporate greed for our highest-in-the-nation gas prices and championing new programs to promote economic justice. Yet when it comes to preparing the state for droughts and fire season, it's a different story. Newsom received some brickbats in 2021 for his claims about the state's level of wildfire preparedness. Capitol Public Radio and NPR—hardly members of the right-wing media— exposed the following in its joint investigation:[35]

[T]he governor has misrepresented his accomplishments and even disinvested in wildfire prevention. The investigation found Newsom overstated, by an astounding 690%, the number of acres treated with fuel breaks and prescribed burns in the very forestry projects he said needed to be prioritized to protect the state's most vulnerable communities. Newsom has claimed that 35 'priority projects' carried out as a result of his executive order resulted in fire prevention work on 90,000 acres. But the state's own data show the actual number is 11,399.

Despite the negative exposure, the administration didn't change course in the ensuing years. Newsom has issued some useful post-wildfire executive orders—ones I'll review in the section on land use and rebuilding efforts—and declared a state of emergency in the affected L.A. communities. But the state has not significantly ramped up its commitment to brush clearance as a means to reduce wildfire risk. We saw the results around Los Angeles.

According to the Legislative Analyst Office's review[36] of the governor's budget items regarding wildfire and forest resilience, "the budget retains $2.6 billion for these activities across an eight-year period (from 2020 through 2028), which is 93% of the multiyear amount originally planned. ... Some other notable changes include reducing $35 million for wildfire resilience projects on state-owned land and reducing $28 million for projects undertaken by various state conservancies. The budget also shifts $164 million for various programs from the General Fund to GGRF and delays the timing of providing that funding." Instead of increasing these priorities, Newsom has been decreasing them. Also consider that miniscule spending in the context of the climate-change budget.

In *The Orange County Register*, Daniel Kolkey, a Pacific Research Institute board member and former California appellate judge, argues the administration ought to shift funding from electric vehicle mandates to forest thinning, prioritize brush clearance in those wildland interface areas, relax renewable energy mandates on utilities so they have the funds to harden power poles, provide tax cuts to homeowners so they can upgrade their homes with fire-resistant materials, and relax timber-harvesting rules to reduce wildfire risk.[37]

At this point, the state needs more than slight tweaks to its forest-clearance approach. This is again from my congressional testimony:[38]

> Regarding brush clearance, the governor has agreed that we need to step up the process. But very little has happened. We need to clear 1 million acres a year per state and federal estimates, but we have averaged only 125,000 acres or less a year. Yet CAL FIRE estimates that the state desperately needs to clear around 15 million acres, 10 million of which are federally owned. As … Kolkey explained in his chapter in the 2021 book *Saving California*, the state's 'progress have been slow and its vision wanting.' Most recent wildfire initiatives have been 'too modest to rise to the challenge.' It's once again a matter of priorities.

It's no small task to maintain California's forests. It requires a federal and state role, as 57% of the state's 33-million forest acres are controlled by the federal government. The pace of forest-restoration efforts here hasn't increased in the past decade. It's widely acknowledged that this must change, but the problem—beyond the state's failure to prioritize it—centers on the regulations that delay and derail the thinning efforts. "Environmental regulations, bureaucratic red tape and litigation risks create obstacles and can delay or derail even the most needed projects," notes the Property and Environment Research Center's Shawn Regan: "Increasing the pace of restoration means cutting red tape, which makes some environmental groups uncomfortable."[39]

That's a gentle way of putting it. We saw how California Coastal Commission approvals delayed a project to upgrade power poles in Pacific Palisades for six years and counting. The California Environmental Quality Act (CEQA) stops not only the construction of housing, but state efforts to undertake forest-thinning projects. Surveys show that 49% of CEQA lawsuits involve environmentally friendly projects.[40] Environmental groups are not just made uncomfortable by such projects—they file lawsuits that delay them, stop them or drive up their cost. Leading politicians count these groups among their political allies, so nothing much happens year after year.

And the number of environmental reviews for such projects—from the state, feds and local agencies—is so daunting that even when an agency has the gumption to try, it gets ground down by the long, bureaucratic process. The state could use money from the Greenhouse Gas Reduction Fund to pay for these projects, rejigger some priorities and commit to stepping up these efforts, but the efforts are for naught if California doesn't permanent-ly reform CEQA and other obstructionist statutes. In June, Newsom muscled the Legislature into passing a broader-based CEQA reform during last-minute budget negotiations. He threatened not to approve the budget without the reform and succeeded. That was admirable, but there is still much more work to do with CEQA.

This isn't exactly a radical notion, even among leading Demo-crats. The governor's own state of emergency proclamation from March 2025 declares that, "State statutes, rules, regulations and requirements that fall within the jurisdiction of boards, departments and offices within the California Environmental Protection Agency and the California Natural Resources Agency are hereby suspended to the extent necessary for expediting critical fuels reduction projects." The proclamation also calls for "rapid environmental review for large wildfire risk reduction treatments."[41]

The governor and Legislature need to resist the demands of environmental activists, who often oppose these clearance projects and committed mainly to imposing development restrictions. This is how the Sierra Club addresses the brush-clearance issue: "The problem lies in focusing state efforts and funds only on the clearing of land, rather than changes to existing buildings, the creation of development requirements, and the effective distribution of well-studied evacuation plans."[42] Meanwhile, the Center for Biological Diversity argues that we should "Stop building new homes in highly fire-prone wildlands."[43] The state won't reduce its wildfire risks and address its housing shortages by continuing along this slow-growth path—and by taking a nonchalant approach toward brush clearance.

The wildfire issue affects other states beyond California, of course. The August 2023 fires in Maui claimed the lives of 102 people. In the aftermath, many officials and experts in Hawaii talked about increasing controlled burns there. "On Maui, we have a history of doing controlled burns," said Joe Kent, of the Grassroot Institute of Hawaii, during a recent Pacific Research Institute podcast. "We had sugar cane for a 100 years and they did controlled burns. The sugar industry went belly up in 2016, leaving the land dry and fallow. That's a wildfire risk," but it's also a "taboo topic" in Hawaii.[44] It's time to make this topic decidedly less taboo in Hawaii and elsewhere.

During a Stanford Institute for Public Policy Research symposium on wildfires (where I spoke about insurance regulations) a professor of fire science at the University of California-Berkeley, Scott Stephens, explained that the state of Western Australia has aggressively embraced prescribed burning in a region with a climate similar to California's. As a result, 80% of the region's land that burns each year is from controlled burns—compared to California, where 95% comes from wildfires. Whatever risks come from controlled burns, they are far less than the ones that come from uncontrolled wildfires.[45] He suggests that California adopt that model as a pilot program in a limited area and see if our state can have similar success.

Regarding CEQA, California officials from both parties recognize its problems. They will only address them on an ad hoc basis. Various laws have exempted or streamlined CEQA provisions for specific types of housing projects—mostly infill and multifamily projects that the state's progressive lawmakers prefer. Politicians routinely exempt CEQA whenever they want to see the construction of a new professional sports arena or high-profile public-works project. But there are no serious efforts to permanently fix an environmental law that serves as an impediment to building—and to environmental improvement.[46]

Because CEQA exemptions have become political footballs in the Legislature, we see some outcomes that seem unfair. For instance, the governor has wisely granted Coastal Act and CEQA exemptions for the Los Angeles rebuilding—but fire victims in Paradise and near Yosemite didn't get the same relaxed treatment. That speaks to the need to just reform those laws for everyone.[47] As my Pacific Research Institute colleague, Tim Anaya, pointed out in PRI's *Right by the Bay* blog, "Newsom did the right thing here, but victims of other recent wildfires, such as the Camp Fire that destroyed Paradise in the North State, are wondering why they weren't afforded the same regulatory relief."

As U.S. Rep. Tom McClintock, R-Elk Grove, said in a speech before Congress:[48] "Draconian restrictions on logging, grazing, prescribed burns and herbicide use on public lands have made modern land management endlessly time-consuming and ultimately cost-prohibitive. A single tree-thinning plan typically takes four years and more than 800 pages of analysis. The costs of this process exceed the value of timber—turning land maintenance from a revenue-generating activity to a revenue-consuming one." If California wants to improve its forest management—and it needs to do so to control the wildfire problem and reach its climate objectives—then it needs to enact more sweeping changes to its landmark environmental law.

Better Water Policy Bolsters Wildfire Prevention

Water policy is only tangentially related to the Los Angeles wildfires, but it's related nonetheless. We saw, as discussed previously, how the long-delayed maintenance on the Santa Ynez Reservoir reduced the amount of water available for fighting fires in the Pacific Palisades.

By most accounts, the state had plenty of water in its reservoirs for this year's wildfire season, but as always the issue centers on efficiently moving water to the right places at the right times.[49]

"Water supply has not hindered firefighting efforts. Reservoirs in California are at or above average storage levels for this time of year, thanks in part to years of proactive water management," according to the Association of California Water Agencies. "There's way more water in local storage than you could ever fight a fire with," said the chief engineer with the Los Angeles Department of Water and Power.[50] These statements are mostly accurate. Indeed, many people, including President Trump, who tried to pin these particular fires on state water policy seemed more interested in scoring political points than in fixing California's water problems. But it would be nice if the governor spent more time trying to fix the many things wrong with the state's water policy and less time reacting to Donald Trump.

As I pointed out in my congressional testimony, "More water would not have stopped the wildfires, but additional water resources would bolster firefighting efforts and mitigate some of the effects of drought seasons. As an aside, the state's limits on natural gas make it hard for water districts to permit generators to move water to where it's needed most. Again, water policy just has not been a state priority with lawmakers pointing fingers at climate change without recognizing policies they could embrace that would mitigate its effects."[51]

In an interview with the Public Policy Institute of California, Wendy Broley, executive director of the California Urban Water Agencies, agreed that the state had enough water for firefighting purposes and pointed out that the current water-infrastructure system is designed to fight structural fires rather than massive wildfires that spread throughout urban neighborhoods. However, she noted that "Climate change is fundamentally changing circumstances, and we do have to adapt. Water is a factor in several climate risks, including drought, flooding, and wildfire."[52]

As I see it, more plentiful water resources would reduce the impact of droughts and, by extension, drought-related wildfires. Brett Barbre of the Yorba Linda Water District concurs: "Droughts come and go, but well-planned infrastructure can mitigate their effects."[53] California has not significantly upgraded its water infrastructure since the 1970s, when the state's population was roughly half of what it is today. Even those voices who say the state had plenty of water to fight fires generally agree that the infrastructure system is outdated and can be greatly improved for firefighting purposes. Of course, the main reason to boost California's water infrastructure is to assure that the state's farms, residents and businesses have enough water to thrive and prosper, but lessening drought conditions and improving fire readiness are useful side benefits.

As I point out in my 2020 Pacific Research Institute book, *Winning the Water Wars*,[54] California built an impressive system of water storage and canals up until the 1970s, but since then embraced an environmentally focused ethic that has prioritized conservation and rationing over infrastructure building. According to state statistics, approximately 50% of California's water flows out to the Pacific, with 40% going to agriculture and only 10% flowing for urban uses. If the state built more reservoirs and invested in desalination and other storage projects, it could capture more water during rainy years and have fewer shortages during dry ones. When it comes to business development, drought or firefighting, more water is better than less.

In the 1957 "California Water Plan," which epitomized the long-abandoned can-do California way of thinking about water infrastructure, state officials laid out a challenge that is even more relevant 68 years later: "Today, the future agricultural, industrial and urban growth of California hinges on a highly important decision, which is well within the power of the people to make. We can move forward with a thriving economy by pursuing a vigorous and progressive water development planning and construction program; or we can allow our economy to stagnate, perhaps even retrogress, by adopting a complacent attitude and leaving each district, community, agency or other entity to secure its own water supply as best it can with small regard to the needs of others."[55]

The state has failed to build new reservoirs. It has also failed to permit many privately funded desalination plants. It has blamed climate change rather than our own complacent policies. The state has unfortunately followed the latter course, but there's always time to change our public-policy priorities. Would a vigorous water-development policy stop the wildfires that have been a fact of life since our state's beginnings? Of course not. But it would mitigate them and make them easier to stop. It's a necessary part of an overall approach that is committed to placing the lives and needs of Californians above the designs of the environmental and no-growth lobbies. The wildfires highlighted how California created a massive administrative state that hobbles its ability to serve the public, so now it's time to dismantle the impediments.

How California Politicians and Voters Destroyed Its Insurance Market

California's failed insurance policies directly affect the state's ability to handle the wildfire challenge. Without a thriving insurance market, California property owners are left vulnerable to wildfire damage—and are unable to quickly rebuild their communities after the destruction. And the state's property insurance system is a certifiable mess. Not many California residents or politicians—including those in the California Department of Insurance—paid much attention to a long-brewing insurance crisis, but then something shocking took place in 2023.

State Farm General Insurance Co. is the state's largest home insurance company, providing nearly 21% of homeowners' policies. It announced that May it would "cease accepting new applications including all business and personal lines property and casualty insurance." It blamed "historic increases in construction costs outpacing inflation, rapidly growing catastrophe exposure, and a challenging reinsurance market."[56] Other insurers followed suit. Without a functioning insurance market, California would face an unprecedented threat to its economy. State officials acted shocked and quickly blamed—drum roll, please—climate change, but they had every reason to see this coming.

Two months before State Farm's announcement, I had reported in *The Wall Street Journal* that California insurers were "quietly" leaving the state.[57] The only difference in May was that given State Farm's share of the market, its announcement was no longer quiet. Two years earlier, I warned in the *American Spectator* that, "In the property insurance area, California insurers had a 13-year string of profitability, but a variety of wildfires in the last few years have led to significant losses. As a result, insurers have stopped renewing policies to many homeowners living in wooded areas. The situation is likely to get worse."[58] And worse it got.

I can't blame the average California homeowner for not paying much attention to problems in the state's complex insurance market. I have less sympathy for the state's politicians, who are responsible for overseeing these markets. I also found it frustrating that so few journalists had covered the issue. Since the Los Angeles wildfires, reporters and commentators nationwide have understandably focused on the problem—but prior to 2023 a reader would find little information about it. That's astounding given that the issue has festered since 1988, although it got much worse in recent years after the spate of wildfires from 2018 to 2020.

In the 1980s, auto insurance premiums were spiraling out of control largely as the result of an infamous 1979 California Supreme Court decision, *Royal Globe v. Superior Court*. As a 2023 report from the International Center for Law & Economics explained, the decision "created precedent that third parties could bring action against a tort-feasor's insurer, even if they were not party to the insurance contract in question. What followed was an explosion in insurance-related litigation, as the number of auto-liability claim filings in California Superior Court rose by 82% between 1980 and 1987, and the severity of claims rose by a factor of four."[59] Auto rates soared and—this being California—voters turned to the initiative process to address the problem.

The state's high court reversed the decision in 1988, but the same year voters faced competing insurance-related initiatives on the statewide ballot. They approved, by a narrow 51%-to-49% vote, arguably the worst of the batch, Proposition 103.[60] Authored by consumer activist Harvey Rosenfield, the measure created a prior-approval insurance system, by which the insurance commissioner had the power to approve rate increases or even demand rate rollbacks. The initiative also turned the insurance commissioner into an elected position, thus creating the incentive for the commissioner to disapprove rate requests. Not many elected officials want to be known as the person who raised voters' insurance rates. Although *Royal Globe* mainly affected auto insurance, voters approved this initiative that applied to auto and property insurance rates.[61]

In a typical market system, companies can charge what they choose and consumers can pick from the products and services offered by competing companies. The competition keeps the rates down. After Prop. 103, insurance companies had to navigate a long and bureaucratic process to get rate hikes. They could ask for no more than 6.9% in one hearing, although the commissioner could mandate a rate reduction if he chose. And insurers were required to pay public "intervenors" who would supposedly represent the public in opposing any such hikes. You're probably not surprised to learn that the main intervenor, which earns millions of dollars from its work, is a group called Consumer Watchdog—the successor group to the one founded by Rosenfield, the initiative's author.

After a series of costly wildfires and unable to adjust rates to reflect risk, insurers then started pulling back from our market. The International Center for Law & Economics continued:[62]

> Prior to the COVID-19 pandemic, California's market was saddled by availability issues stemming from a series of historically costly wildfires. California homeowners' insurers posted a combined underwriting loss of $20 billion for the massive wildfire years of 2017 and 2018 alone, more than double the total combined underwriting profit of $10 billion that the state's homeowners' insurers had generated from 1991 to 2016. Partly in response to those losses, as well as the inability to adjust rates expeditiously, the numberof non-renewals of California residential-property policies grew by 36% in 2019, and new policies written by the state's residual-market FAIR Plan surged 225% that same year.

The FAIR Plan stands for Fair Access to Insurance Requirements. It's the state-created, industry funded, bare-bones insurer of last resort. Because insurers have been fleeing, many of the Los Angeles wildfire victims were uninsured, underinsured or dependent on this "it's better than nothing, but not by much" insurance program. There's now much talk of its possible insolvency, which would further burden insurers (who must bail it out partly based on the share of the market in the state), which would then encourage more of them to flee. It's a potential death spiral.

The state in February 2025 allowed the plan to impose $1 billion of assessments on insurance companies to keep it afloat, but as the *New York Times* reported,[63] that "move is likely to drive up insurance costs for homeowners across the state" and "marks a perilous new stage for California's home insurance market," as the bailout increases pressure on insurers to leave. It's hard to quickly fix an insurance market that's been on shaky ground for so many years.

There is some hopeful news. Democratic Insurance Commissioner Ricardo Lara received intense (and well-deserved) criticism for his inexplicable state-funded luxury travel to conferences and whatnot across the globe. Nevertheless, he implemented some of the main reforms that the industry had called for over the years. They basically allow insurers to charge rates that better reflect market conditions and their risk. Almost everyone at this point realizes that higher-priced policies are better for consumers than no available policies.

First, Lara's Sustainable Insurance Strategy[64] allowed insurers to use catastrophe models, which only makes sense if climate change is the huge problem that state officials claim. Instead of relying on past claims history to predict future losses, this allows them to take into account higher risks stemming from a potentially hotter climate. Second, it allows insurers to factor rising reinsurance rates into their premiums. Reinsurance is the insurance that insurance companies buy. By using it to protect their assets, they can write more policies—and that's exactly what California needs now: more policies. Reinsurance costs have been rising.

As I wrote in *The Orange County Register*,[65] "Lara is speeding up the rate-review process, which has become a time-consuming, costly and frustrating mess. He's pushing for a 60-day review timeline—and came up with a realistic plan that forces insurance-department officials to provide detailed reasons if they can't meet that timeline." He shored up the FAIR Plan and—at one of his junkets to a reinsurance conference in Bermuda—promised to tackle outsized intervenor fees, noting that intervenors hold the rate process hostage. He's approved every rate increase proposed by the insurance companies. The commissioner didn't do much until the crisis hit and previously implemented some disastrously bad policies (including one that pushed a major auto insurer out of the state), but these policies ought to stave off an industry collapse. Indeed, seven insurers have since announced expanding underwriting in the state. It's too early to express relief, but there's reason for hope.[66]

Despite the progress, this is an asinine system to determine the rates of what ultimately is just a product, albeit a very important one. The proper role of insurance regulation is to make sure that companies who offer insurance have the wherewithal to pay claims—and to make sure they do indeed pay all legitimate claims. Rate setting is not an appropriate role. It amounts to a price control. Wherever price controls have been imposed, shortages (and then higher prices) follow. Gasoline price controls led to gas lines. Insurance price controls lead to property owners becoming uninsured, underinsured or dependent on a financially teetering FAIR Plan or on surplus-lines companies that operate with little oversight.

Now that the rebuilding process begins, California needs to reform its insurance laws so that homeowners and businesses can access the policies they need to move forward. And, as a speaker at the Stanford conference noted, the lack of insurance can destroy the mortgage market, too, as no company will underwrite a mortgage on a property that can't get fire coverage.[67] Will the state undertake such important work? If the past is a guide, it's hard to be optimistic.

Land Use, Housing and Rebuilding Regulations

After the wildfires began their devastation, Newsom issued an executive order[68] that wisely exempted rebuilding efforts in the devastated areas from state environmental regulations. The two key provisions are unobjectionable. The first would "Suspend CEQA review and California Coastal Act permitting for reconstruction of properties substantially damaged or destroyed in recent Southern California wildfires." The second would "Direct state agencies to identify additional permitting requirements, including provisions of the Building Code that can safely be suspended or streamlined to accelerate rebuilding and make it more affordable." The fourth, although vague, also is admirable as the governor committed to "working with the Legislature to identify statutory changes that can help expedite rebuilding while enhancing wildfire resilience and safety."

The order's third item—"extend protections against price gouging on building materials, storage services, construction, and other essential goods and services to Jan. 7, 2026, in Los Angeles County"[69]—is counterproductive. When items are in short supply, allowing prices to fluctuate to reflect their scarcity is the best way to get materials into the disaster zone quickly. Prices will moderate as supplies increase. But, nevertheless, three out of four isn't bad—especially in an administration not exactly known for its embrace of market economics.

Newsom followed up with a series of orders—good and bad, but mostly good—that expedited debris clearance, fast-tracking government relief and further expediting local regulatory exemptions. "We will not let overly strict regulations get in the way of rebuilding these communities," he said. "The state stands with its local partners to ensure that we cut red tape and make recovery as easy as possible."[70] There's no arguing with his words, although it seems unlikely that they are enough to chip away at years of burgeoning regulatory barriers.

As mentioned earlier, state officials have long known about the impediments placed in the way of housing construction and infrastructure by CEQA and the Coastal Act. The state is in the midst of a housing crisis, as statewide median home prices have soared above $800,000 as of June 2025. Most market-rate developments, which require discretionary governmental approvals, are subject to the long and costly Environmental Impact Report process—and frequently are targeted by CEQA lawsuits. A private firm had proposed building a water desalination plant at an industrial site in Orange County that would have met the needs of 10% of the county's residents, but the commission unanimously rejected the projects after years of debate and discussion over fears about its effect on ocean plankton around the intake valves. Newsom supported the project, but alas his commission appointees did not.[71]

Regarding housing, California Democrats have led the charge over several years for various housing bills that have, in a limited manner, streamlined CEQA requirements for housing. Senate Bill 423[72], signed in 2023, created CEQA exemptions to build housing in cities that comply with the state's housing man-dates—and even applied to cities in the coastal zone. Senate Bills 9 and 10[73] are other landmark housing laws. SB 9 creates a "by right" housing approval for duplexes in single-family neighbor-hoods and SB 10 does so for multi-family projects along housing routes. SB 9 is caught up in the courts.

We're already seeing a battle over what gets built to replace what was destroyed. PRI fellow Kerry Jackson fears that Los Angeles officials will be tempted to rebuild the burned-out mostly single-family neighborhoods along the lines of the city's master plan. That means design standards that "positively transform the urban environment," and "require careful strategic planning and investment" to create "intelligent urban ecosystems designed for the humans that live there."[74] In English, it means higher densities.

So far, the approach taken by the city and county seems fo-cused on rebuilding along the "fire-wise" principles that incor-porate best practices in wildfire resilience. I braced for the worst when I saw an article in the environmentalist planning publi-cation, *Planetizen*, which reported on rebuilding resources from the county's Chief Sustainability Office and its climate resilience officer. But, per the article,[75] the office is mainly concerned about making sure "practices like building hardening and defensible space not only help individual properties but significantly im-prove neighborhood-scale resilience."

An article in the left-wing *Nation* magazine[76] focused on dev-astation in Altadena in the San Gabriel Valley, a city settled by African Americans who fled the discrimination of the Jim Crow South. To its credit, the publication's concern—a legitimate one, in my view—was assuring that residents there had the resources and help necessary to rebuild their community in ways that re-

LAND USE, HOUSING AND REBUILDING REGULATIONS

flected the history of the city. For instance, architects are "compiling a set of plans for the types of houses typically found in Altadena—ranches, Mission style, Craftsman bungalows—and working with other architects (and, ideally, builders) to streamline the design and construction process so that displaced residents can rebuild as quickly and easily as possible."[77]

That's great. But there are plenty of reasons to share Jackson's concern. As Reuters reported,[78] "As Los Angeles recovers from its devastating wildfires, environmental engineers, urban planners and natural disaster experts are casting forward with visions of what could come next for neighborhoods that have been reduced to ash and rubble. Apartment buildings could spring up where strip malls and parking lots once stood, with locals walking to ground-floor shops, offices and cafes, European-style." The headline calls it a "moonshot moment"—but Los Angeles needs fewer moonshots and more policies that uphold property owners' rights to rebuild their homes as they please.

So far, most of the re-envisioning talk is just that, talk. Beyond the state exemptions from CEQA and the Coastal Act, the city of Los Angeles has waived a controversial rule that required new construction to be electric-only—overturning a ban on natural-gas appliances. Furthermore, the city is taking a lenient approach toward "non-conforming" structures, thus allowing them to be rebuilt as before as long as they don't exceed 110% of the pre-existing size.[79] The myriad exemptions give wide latitude for affected homeowners to rebuild, which reduces concerns that planning agencies might use the destruction as an opportunity to force a change in local land-use patterns. But we'll watch and see.

If California is ever going to address its housing shortages, it needs to take lessons from the wildfires and get serious about reforming CEQA. The wildfires reinforced that these regulations are impediments to construction. Four months after the devastation, we're still not seeing calls for overturning or revising the 1970 law, but lawmakers are going further than before. "The effort by two Bay Area lawmakers to exempt most urban housing developments from the state's premier environmental regulation—an idea that has drawn some of the state's most powerful interest groups into a fierce legislative debate—just received a prized endorsement from Gov. Gavin Newsom," *CalMatters* reported.[80] It's only one step in the right direction—and the measure applies only to urban housing—but it is progress. That's perhaps one of the few silver linings from the wildfires.

Private Approaches Toward Improving Resilience

When officials evaluate the wildfire response, they often overlook the role of private property owners, private homeowners' associations and even private insurers in mitigating the ill effects of these dangers. Sure they talk about imposing fire-wise building standards and mull over troubles in the insurance market, but they generally view property owners and companies as people and industries to be cajoled and regulated—rather than as crucial partners (actually, the leaders) in the process.

Perhaps the strangest example of this came after news reports showed that some wealthy Angelenos had hired private firefighters to protect their homes and businesses. "While private firefighting in the U.S. dates back to the 1700s, the controversial industry has come under renewed scrutiny," according to a January 2025 article in *CalMatters*.[81] They primarily "visit the homes of typically wealthy clientele as a fire approaches and take preventive measures." For instance, former mayoral candidate Rick Caruso's Palisades Village shopping center was saved by a team of private firefighters—something that caused a social-media backlash given Caruso's wealth and politics. Democrats in the Legislature even tried to ban private firefighters from using public hydrants—a shameful measure that was more about class envy and union job protections than improving wildfire protection.[82]

It's amazing that such a thing could be controversial, given that this is, after all, a country that still values private enterprise. More than half of the nation's firefighters are volunteers.[83] And the state relies heavily on volunteer prison firefighters who earn a pittance. "But critics argue these companies create a two-tiered system where the haves get better protection than the have-nots," the article continues. "By law, private firefighters are also supposed to coordinate with local incident commanders, but during the wildfire seasons in 2007 and 2017, there were reports of private firefighters entering disaster zones without proper coordination, which confused residents and distracted emergency responders."[84]

That's just crazy. In these cases, the fires were out of control. Any additional help was useful. It's strange to argue that it's wrong to put out fires at some people's houses because those people can afford better protection than others. It's even more counterproductive to complain that private firefighters, who are generally as well trained as public firefighters, should stop what they're doing unless they submit to whatever coordination plans are offered by bureaucratic officials.

The real reason for the anger (beyond the usual class-warfare sentiments involves union job protection. The various firefighters' unions are powerful in Sacramento. The median total compensation of a state firefighter is around $200,000 a year, with median compensation for municipal firefighters much higher than that. Transparent California data shows that some LA firefighters earned total compensation packages above $800,000 and even $900,000.[85] That's extraordinarily generous—a testament to union power, which translates the public's support for firefighters into enviable pay packages. That power is particularly pronounced in local governments, where police and fire are the most muscular political players. They often act in a brazen manner.

"California lawmakers have introduced a bill to ban private firefighters, like those who saved many buildings in the Palisades and Eaton fires, from using public hydrants, saying firefighting is a 'public good,'" reported Kenneth Schrupp in *The Center Square*. "Assemblyman Isaac Bryan, D-Los Angeles, introduced Assembly Bill 1075 with the support of the California Professional Firefighters Union, which claims private firefighters are not trained or equipped as well. 'They don't train to the same standards,' said CPF President Brian Rice to *Politico* regarding the bill. 'They're not equipped like we are. They're not professionals like we are.'"[86] It reminds me of the tactics firefighters' unions and their political backers pulled to stop cities from creating their own fire departments as a way to stretch their budgets and boost response times.[87] The key proposal involved switching to a defined-contribution pension system, so the union went to the Legislature (and got a Republican author) to kill any such local efforts. It's all about protecting their sky-high pay and pensions—even if it means hobbling city budgets or keeping private firefighters from helping with the wildfire effort.

Some wealthy people and companies did hire pricey private firefighters. Why not, as it's better than letting millions of dollars of property to incinerate and possibly take other properties with them? But the bulk of them are hired by insurance companies, which use them to protect average citizens' properties and thus reduce insurance losses. It's "a standard part of homeowner policies in fire-prone states—and in California, they operate under state regulations," NPR reported.[88] They're perfectly legal, work with state agencies and most of their work is fire prevention, as they remove debris and other combustible materials prior to any encroaching fire. What's wrong with that? In fact, insurance inspectors play a key role in fire protection as they inspect properties and require property owners to reduce hazards—something they must do or lose their policy.

Many homeowners want to harden their properties against fire hazards, in particular by clearing brush surrounding the house. However, such efforts often need multiple permits. I reviewed one typical fact sheet[89] from a local government, San Diego County, and it contained a lengthy list of permits, considerations and approvals that property owners need before clearing out fire hazards. State officials are looking at ways to promote fire-wise building and retrofit standards, but it would help to first remove the obstacles for sensible brush clearance at private residences.

Basically everyone agrees that such standards are useful. They emphasize using fire-retardant building materials, creating a defensible space around the structure and landscaping in a manner that reduces wildfire risk. In some cases, homeowner associations can lead the efforts. In the Sierra Nevada Mountains around Truckee, the Donner Tahoe Association[90] represents 25,000 people with 6,500 homes in the dense forests around Lake Tahoe. For decades, the association has actively managed area forests and has imposed strictly enforced fire-wise covenants, which assures that area's homes aren't consumed by routine wildfires.

In May 2025, the *Sierra Sun* reported on a "groundbreaking move that could reshape wildfire insurance nationwide" as "the Tahoe Donner Association has secured a first-of-its-kind policy that links premium pricing directly to decades of active forest management."[91] In other words, as California struggles through an insurance crisis that is leaving many homeowners—especially those in wooded areas—without affordable plans or any insurance at all, a major insurer is providing extensive affordably priced policies to a subdivision in the midst of a fire-prone area because of the fire-prevention efforts that subdivision's HOA has in place. There are lessons here.

As usual, California lawmakers need to stop viewing every problem solely through the lens of the public sector and come up with ways to incentivize private homeowners and businesses to mitigate their fire risks. At the very least, the Legislature and local governments need to get out of the way and let private property owners, associations and companies implement best practices.

Conclusion: Is There Reason for Post-Wildfire Optimism?

Following the wildfires, the governor issued his emergency executive orders, but the Legislature also has been putting together a package of bills. In April, Newsom signed a bill that earmarks $170 million to nature conservancies to focus on land management.[92] In February, Senate President Pro Tempore Mike McGuire, D-Healdsburg, introduced a package called the Golden State Commitment that promises a wide range of wildfire-prevention, recovery and response measures.

These include, per the senator's statement, bills (approved by the Senate on June 3, 2025) that "Speed-up residential rebuilds; provide property tax relief; protect consumers from price gouging; expand insurance protections for small businesses; expand protections for homeowners, tenants, and mobile home residents; support the rebuilding of health facilities; strengthen penalties against bad actors following disasters; provide desperately needed resources for impacted school districts; transition all 3,000 seasonal CAL FIRE firefighters to full-time, permanent status; establish an insurance community hardening commission that will ensure more fire-safe communities and homeowners get the financial credit they deserve; advance new policies that require fire-safe landscaping, setbacks, and inspections in high fire hazard zones."[93]

As you can imagine, this mish-mash of priorities includes useful measures that reduce rebuilding hurdles and provide tax relief, economically illiterate ones that forbid "price-gouging" and unsolicited offers for properties, giveaways to firefighter unions, and decent ones that promote fire-wise building standards. Still, this being California, there's nothing totally awful in the package or the governor's executive actions—and some positive movement toward limiting building regulations. It's more good news than bad. Same goes on the insurance front. The situation remains troubling, but the latest insurance regulations move in the right direction—and we're seeing a few companies increasing their presence in our market. It shouldn't have taken a crisis to force the governor, insurance commissioner and Legislature to act, but at least they did finally act.

Los Angeles politicians have yet to face their voters over their wildfire preparation and response, but they should worry. Even notoriously progressive San Francisco has self-corrected to some degree. Voters elected a more moderate new mayor, tougher-on-crime district attorney (after recalling their progressive DA), non-leftist school board members and passed some conservative-leaning ballot measures.[94] It was largely a backlash against the city's increasing crime and public disorder. Simmering anger over the mishandling of major wildfires could spark a backlash in the city of Los Angeles and Los Angeles County. We'll see if it happens, but it's not an outlandish thought that the fires were enough of a shock to the local political system to usher in reform-minded leadership.

After wading through the reams of misinformation, false narratives, conspiracy theories and hobby horsing that followed the wildfires, economics blogger Noah Smith came to some useful conclusions: "(I)f you remained calm, resisted the urge to dunk on your political enemies, and watched the situation unfold, I think there were a few important signals you could extract … . Basically, the lessons I take away from the horrific L.A. fires are: The insurance industry as we know it is in big trouble. Climate change is making wildfires worse, but there's not much we can do about that right now. Forest management needs to get a lot more proactive, but is being blocked by regulation. Wildfire preparedness is just a lot more important than it used to be."[95]

That's fairly obvious, but is a good summary of the key takeaways. State leaders understand the first point and actually are making some progress on it. They refuse to acknowledge the second point, even if virtually everyone else understands the limits of the state's climate-change policies. There's little disagreement on the third and the fourth points. So that's progress. Understanding the situation isn't a solution, but it's the foundation for finding one.

Having watched governors and Legislatures drop the ball time and again in my decades writing about our state government, I won't say that I'm optimistic that state lawmakers will learn the right lessons from the Los Angeles wildfires. But I am optimistic that LA will rebuild relatively quickly (thanks mainly to the energy of the private sector), that the insurance market will eventually bounce back, that urbanists won't have too big of a hand in how the city is rebuilt, and that we'll at least see more discussions in the Legislature about reforming CEQA and other building impediments, albeit on a limited basis. While the situation could be worse, it could be much better. Here is a summary of some of the policy takeaways from this booklet.

Battling governmental incompetence: This is perhaps the toughest reform area, as there is no easy button to improve governance. The voters make their choice—and it's not always easy to increase oversight and accountability, especially in cities with little partisan competition. However, the depth of public anger following the Los Angeles wildfires could jump-start political debates in the city, which is always a healthy outcome. However, California cities are long overdue for debating the nature of their union-dominated employment systems. Lost in the fight between Mayor Bass and former Fire Chief Crowley was the degree to which union priorities drive spending policies. Cities such as Los Angeles need to reform their pension systems, their overtime rules and other employee compensation issues. By achieving cost savings in these areas, they can have more money to earmark for additional firefighting—and even hire more firefighters.

Improving brush clearance: California's brush-clearance efforts are inadequate and mired in layers of state and local bureaucracy. For starters, the state needs to step up its funding for these efforts—and not just pay lip service to their importance. This doesn't require new expenditures, but merely prioritizing them among the long list of spending programs included in California's $325-billion budget. The state could, for instance, shift funding from electric vehicle mandates to forest thinning and relax utilities' renewable energy mandates to encourage them to harden power poles. I also mentioned the need for tax cuts for homeowners to help them upgrade to fire-resistant materials. The state should reduce its timber-harvesting rules to encourage private brush clearance. And CEQA is always the elephant in the room. The state should completely overhaul (or overturn) this environmental law, which impedes brush clearance and almost every other project. Lawmakers should consider a pilot project—similar to the one I mentioned in Western Australia—that reduces the potential for wildfires by aggressively promoting proscribed burns in a targeted region.

Better water policy: This was the subject of my 2020 PRI book, *Winning the Water Wars*. Basically, California needs to get serious about increasing its capacity to store water—and not rely solely on conservation, which provides only diminishing returns, and on managing scarcity. The state should permit privately funded desalination plants, complete Sites Reservoir (a long-planned off-stream storage facility north of Sacramento), expand its water-recycling program modeled on Orange County's nation-leading efforts, loosen regulations that restrict water trading and store more water during rainy years so we have it during droughts. Completing the Delta tunnel(s) project could reduce delays in sending water from Tracy to farms and cities southward. California needs to prioritize abundance and—here it is again—further reform CEQA, so no-growth activists can't delay or stop every proposed water project.

Enacting insurance reforms: California has belatedly enacted many of the insurance reforms that are needed to improve property insurance availability. It has sped up the rate-review process, taken steps to shore up the FAIR Plan, allowed insurers to factor rising reinsurance rates into their premium pricing and allowed insurers to use catastrophe modeling to set prices. The Department of Insurance has approved almost every recent rate hike that's come before it—a necessary albeit painful approach to keep insurers from fleeing and further overburdening the FAIR Plan. But, ultimately, the state needs to revisit Proposition 103, the

1988 ballot initiative that imposed a prior-approval rate system that amounts to a system of price controls. Until the state's voters reform this at the ballot box, California's insurance market will not function effectively or efficiently. And shortages will remain.

Rethinking land-use regulations: While I applaud Gov. Newsom's decision to exempt Los Angeles fire victims from the Coastal Act and CEQA and his efforts to push through CEQA reform during budget negotiations, I'm frustrated that the state Legislature never undertakes broad-based, permanent reform of the latter (the former would need to go to the ballot box). CEQA continues to impede every type of construction. Five years after a fire that demolished the town, Paradise—which never received such useful exemptions—has not been fully rebuilt. Even with the LA exemptions, the rebuilding process is slow, with only 30 permits so far approved in the two main wildfire areas as of June 2025 per the state's dashboard. This speaks to the large amount of bureaucracy in the city and county. Local officials need to find ways to streamline these building approvals.

Prioritizing privatization: California's state and local officials continue to choose government approaches as their first-reach answer to everything. They often dismiss—or even actively oppose, in the case of private firefighters—efforts that unleash the most energetic part of our economy, the private sector. This "reform" requires more of a change in perspective than any particular policy. But the state could encourage the creation of homeowners' associations, such as the one described at the Tahoe-Donner Association. Despite being in the midst of a fire-prone forest, that community has resisted devastating fires by implementing a variety of private restrictions and building requirements. I'd urge

California lawmakers to look at these private-sector approaches and find ways to promote them in other communities statewide.

California has done some of the right things after the latest wildfires, but it's taken an unprecedented disaster to prod state officials into taking even modest productive steps forward. Let's hope the Los Angeles tragedy will indeed serve as a wakeup call and that state lawmakers don't just go back to business as usual after it fades from the public's memory.

Endnotes

1   Natalia Osuna, "Here is a timeline of the Eaton and Palisades Fires in LA County," NBC Los Angeles, Jan. 24, 2025, www.nbclosangeles.com/news/california-wildfires/timeline-eaton-palisades-fires-la-county/3614940/

2   Staff, "California fires: Facts, FAQs, and how to help," World Vision, www.worldvision.org/disaster-relief-news-stories/california-fires-facts-faqs-how-to-help, accessed May 31, 2025.

3   Roger Vincent, "Estimated Cost of Fire Damage Balloons to More than $250 Billion," *Los Angeles Times,* Jan. 24, 2025, https://www.latimes.com/business/story/2025-01-24/estimated-cost-of-fire-damage-balloons-to-more-than-250-billion

4   Janie Har and Jocelyn Gecker, "Victims of the Paradise wildfire; stunning portraits of how they lived and died," Associated Press, Feb. 22, 2019, https://www.ap.org/news-highlights/best-of-the-states/2019/stories-of-the-paradise-wildfire-victims/

5   Staff, "History of California Wildfires," Western Fire Chiefs Association, Nov. 17, 2022, www.wfca.com/wildfire-articles/history-of-california-wildfires/

6   Ibid.

7   "Our Changing Population: California," USA Facts, www.usafacts.org/data/topics/people-society/population-and-demo-graphics/our-changing-population/state/california/, accessed May 31, 2025.

8   Alejandro Lazo, "CA may force companies to disclose climate impacts," *CalMatters*, June 27, 2023, www.calmatters.org/environment/climate-change/2023/06/california-legislation-corporate-climate-change/

9   Staff, "Wildfires are erasing California's climate gains, UChicago research shows," UChicago News, Oct. 25, 2022, https://news.uchicago.edu/story/wildfires-are-erasing-californias-climate-gains-research-shows

10 Steven Greenhut, "Testimony, Hearing on "California Fires and the Consequences of Overregulation" - R Street Institute," Feb. 6, 2025, www.rstreet.org/outreach/steven-greenhut-testimony-hearing-on-california-fires-and-the-consequences-of-overregulation/

11 Staff, "America's Urban Wildfire Crisis," Headwaters Economics, Feb. 26, 2025, www.headwaterseconomics.org/wildfire/more-than-1100-communities-urban-wildfire-risk/

12 Staff, "History of California Wildfires," Western Fire Chiefs Association, Nov. 17, 2022, www.wfca.com/wildfire-articles/history-of-california-wildfires/

13 California YIMBY, "The Impact of Land Use Planning on Wildfire Risk: A Study in Southern California," www.cayimby.org/blog/the-impact-of-land-use-planning-on-wildfire-risk-a-study-in-southern-california/, accessed May 31, 2025.

14 Randal O'Toole, "Smart Growth Burns Thousands of Homes," *New Geography,* Jan. 21, 2025, www.newgeography.com/content/008416-smart-growth-burns-thousands-homes

15 Staff, "In Altadena, loss extends far beyond homes," Community Organization Relief Effort (CORE), https://www.coreresponse.org/post/in-altadena-the-losses-go-far-beyond-homes/, accessed May 31, 2025

16 Matt Craig, "Joan Didion Said It Best," No Content for Old Men Substack, Jan. 9, 2025, https://mattcraig.substack.com/p/joan-didion-said-it-best

17 2025 QLI Final Report, https://ucla.app.box.com/s/5h-q7trv75z30snqjidfmj2ufd2h6ctpc, accessed May 31, 2025.

18 David K. Li, "Video shows Mayor Karen Bass refusing to answer L.A. fire questions as she returns from trip abroad," NBC News, Jan. 9, 2025, https://www.nbcnews.com/news/us-news/video-shows-mayor-karen-bass-refuse-answer-l-fires-questions-returns-t-rcna186957

19 Jonathan Vigliotti and Kelsie Hoffman, "Leadership in L.A. facing backlash over accountability after devastating wildfires," CBS News, Feb. 25, 2025, https://www.cbsnews.com/news/leadership-los-angeles-backlash-accountability-wildfires/

20 Jonathan Vigliotti, "Leadership in L.A. facing backlash over accountability after devastating wildfires," CBS News, Feb. 25, 2025, https://www.cbsnews.com/news/leadership-los-angeles-backlash-accountability-wildfires/

21 Kristin Crowley memo to Los Angeles' Board of Fire Commissioners, Dec. 24, 2024, https://clkrep.lacity.org/onlinedocs/2024/24-1600_rpt_bfc_12-17-24.pdf

22 David Zahniser, "Did Mayor Karen Bass really cut the fire department budget? The answer gets tricky," Jan. 10, 2025, *Los Angeles Times,* https://www.latimes.com/california/story/2025-01-10/how-much-did-the-l-a-fire-department-really-cut-its-budget

23 Matt Hamilton and David Zahniser, "This reservoir was built to save Pacific Palisades. It was empty when the flames came," *Los Angeles Times,* https://www.latimes.com/california/story/2025-01-22/why-has-a-reservoir-in-palisades-stood-empty-for-a-year

24 Ibid.

25 Ross Palombo, "KCAL News investigation finds more than 1,300 fire hydrants need maintenance across LA," KCAL News, Feb. 12, 2025, www.cbsnews.com/losangeles/news/kcal-news-investigation-finds-more-than-1300-fire-hydrants-need-maintenance-across-la/

26 Ian James, Matt Hamilton and Ruben Vives, "Why hydrants ran dry as firefighters battled California's deadly fires," *Los Angeles Times,* Jan. 10, 2025, https://www.latimes.com/environment/story/2025-01-09/california-fires-water-supply-problems

27 Steven Malanga, "LA's Total Leadership Failure," *City Journal,* Jan. 10, 2025, https://www.city-journal.org/article/la-mayor-karen-bass-budget-wildfires

28 Transparent California database, https://transparentcalifornia.com/

29 Scott Beyer, "Los Angeles Pension Problem is Robbing the City," April 25, 2018, *The Market Urbanist,* www.marketurbanist.com/blog/los-angeles-pension-problem-is-robbing-the-city

30 Alex Oliveira, "California bureaucrats halted Pacific Palisades fire safety project to save endangered shrub," *New York Post,* Jan. 14, 2025, www.nypost.com/2025/01/14/us-news/california-bureaucrats-halted-pacific-palisades-fire-safety-project-to-save-endangered-shrub/

31 Sophie Clark, "Endangered Plant May Have Made California Wildfires Worse," *Newsweek,* Jan. 16, 2025, www.newsweek.com/endangered-plant-pacific-palisades-fire-2016053

32 Ian James and Matt Hamilton, "Newsom orders investigation into dry fire hydrants during L.A. fires," *Los Angeles Times,* Jan. 10, 2025, www.latimes.com/environment/story/2025-01-10/newsom-water-fires-investigation

33 California Budget 2025-26, https://ebudget.ca.gov/

34 California Budget 2023-24, "Climate Change," https://ebudget.ca.gov/2023-24/pdf/Enacted/BudgetSummary/ClimateChange.pdf

35 Scott Rodd, "Newsom Misled The Public About Wildfire Prevention Efforts Ahead Of Worst Fire Season On Record," Capradio, June 23, 2021, https://www.capradio.org/articles/2021/06/23/newsom-misled-the-public-about-wildfire-prevention-efforts-ahead-of-worst-fire-season-on-record/

36 Staff," The 2024-25 California Spending Plan, Resources and Environmental Protection," Legislative Analyst's Office, https://lao.ca.gov/Publications/Report/4928

37 Daniel Kolkey, Enough virtue-signaling: 5 tangible ways Newsom can reduce wildfire risk," *The Orange County Register,* May 12, 2025, www.ocregister.com/2025/05/12/enough-virtue-signaling-5-tangible-ways-newsom-can-reduce-wildfire-risk/

38 Steven Greenhut, "Testimony, Hearing on "California Fires and the Consequences of Overregulation" - R Street Institute," Feb. 6, 2025, www.rstreet.org/outreach/steven-greenhut-testimony-hearing-on-california-fires-and-the-consequences-of-overregulation/

39 Shawn Regan, "California's Wildfire Crisis," Property and Environment Research Center, April 7, 2021, https://www.perc.org/2021/04/07/californias-wildfire-crisis/

40 Jennifer Hernandez and David Friedman, "In the Name of the Environment: Litigation Abuse Under CEQA," Holland & Knight, August 2015, https://www.hklaw.com/en/insights/publications/2015/08/in-the-name-of-the-environment-litigation-abuse-un

41 Office of Gov. Gavin Newsom, "Governor Newsom signs executive order to build Los Angeles back faster, prevent future fires," March 27, 2025, https://www.gov.ca.gov/2025/03/27/governor-newsom-signs-executive-order-to-build-los-angeles-back-faster-prevent-future-fires/

42 Amy Murre, "Wildfire Protections for Homes," Sierra Club California, www.sierraclub.org/california/cnrcc/wildfire-protections-for-homes, accessed May 31, 2025.

43 Tiffany Yap, J.P. Rose et al., "Built to Burn," February 2021, https://www.biologicaldiversity.org/programs/urban/pdfs/Built-to-Burn-California-Wildfire-Report-Center-Biological-Diversity.pdf

44 Pacific Research Institute *Next Round* podcast, Feb. 11, 2025, https://www.pacificresearch.org/joe-kent-lessons-from-maui-as-la-begins-to-rebuild/

45 Krysten Crawford, "Who's paying the price for California's wildfires? 'Everyone.'," Stanford Institute for Economic Policy Research (SIEPR), https://siepr.stanford.edu/news/whos-paying-price-californias-wildfires-everyone\

46 Steven Greenhut, "Lawmakers know CEQA is a bust, so why won't they fix it?" *The Orange County Register,* April 25, 2025, https://www.ocregister.com/2025/04/25/lawmakers-know-ceqa-is-a-bust-so-why-wont-they-fix-it/

47 Tim Anaya, "Newsom Right to Waive CEQA for Wildfire Rebuilding, But Lawmakers Should Also Act," *Right by the Bay,* Pacific Research Institute, Jan. 16, 2025, https://www.pacificresearch.org/newsom-right-to-waive-ceqa-for-wildfire-rebuilding-but-lawmakers-should-also-act/

48 Edward Ring and Steve Hilton, "Modern Forest Management," California Policy Center, March 15, 2025, www.californiapolicycenter.org/reports/reducing-californias-carbon-emissions-through-modern-forest-management/

49 Office of Gov. Gavin Newsom, "Hear the experts give the real facts on California water," https://www.gov.ca.gov/2025/01/27/hear-the-experts-give-the-real-facts-on-california-water/

50 Ibid.

51 Steven Greenhut, "Lawmakers know CEQA is a bust, so why won't they fix it?" *The Orange County Register,* April 25, 2025, https://www.ocregister.com/2025/04/25/lawmakers-know-ce-qa-is-a-bust-so-why-wont-they-fix-it/

52 Sarah Bardeen, "The Challenges of Fighting Wildfires with Urban Water Systems," the Public Policy Institute of California, Feb. 19, 2025, www.ppic.org/blog/the-challenges-of-fighting-wildfires-with-urban-water-systems/

53 Brett Barbre, "Fires and the Future," California Insider, https://californiainsider.com/california-news/californi-as-water-crisis-infrastructure-fires-and-the-future-an-inter-view-with-brett-barbre-5799514

54 Steven Greenhut, *Winning the Water Wars: California can meet its water needs by promoting abundance rather than managing scarcity,* Pacific Research Institute, 2020, https://www.amazon.com/Winning-Water-Wars-California-promoting/dp/0936488077

55 Ibid.

56 State Farm Newsroom, "State Farm General Insurance Company: California New Business Update," May 26, 2023, https://https://newsroom.statefarm.com/state-farm-general-insur-ance-company-california-new-business-update/

57 Steven Greenhut, "Insurers Quietly Leaving California," *Wall Street Journal,* March 17, 2023, https://www.wsj.com/articles/insurance-companies-are-quietly-fleeing-california-proposi-tion-103-natural-disaster-state-farm-market-competition-ri-

cardo-lara-commissioner-db0af00?gaa_at=eafs&gaa_n=AS-
WzDAjBlvaZjNvVAjJ2NcIp12pS1yQvirwSkSput8_XD-
DucdSDPLb31bvyul5aaMDU%3D&gaa_ts=683b91dc&gaa_
sig=uo9V-6kozyyG-S2gDVGcfQwc0MgjgPy1eDFqWXWA-
j98GoYGXVd7qqiNvA_EcYOa7CivPDiMtUCSB_fujtA-
5aUg%3D%3D

58   Steven Greenhut, "Insuring Another Disaster, *American Spectator*, April 30, 2021, https://www.rstreet.org/commentary/
insuring-another-disaster/

59   Lawrence Powell, R.J. Lehmann and Ian Adams, "Rethinking
Prop. 103's Approach to Insurance Regulation," International
Center for Law & Economics, Nov. 6. 2023, https://lawecon-
center.org/resources/rethinking-prop-103s-approach-to-insur-
ance-regulation/

60   California Department of Insurance, "Prop 103 Consumer
Intervenor Process," https://www.insurance.ca.gov/01-con-
sumers/150-other-prog/01-intervenor/, accessed May 31, 2025

61   Lawrence Powell, R.J. Lehmann and Ian Adams, "Rethinking
Prop. 103's Approach to Insurance Regulation," International
Center for Law & Economics, Nov. 6. 2023, https://lawecon-
center.org/resources/rethinking-prop-103s-approach-to-insur-
ance-regulation/

62   Ibid.

63   Christopher Flavelle, "California's FAIR Plan Gets $1 Billion
Bailout After L.A. Fires," *New York Times*, Feb. 11, 2025, www.
nytimes.com/2025/02/11/climate/california-fairplan-insur-
ance-bailout.html

64 California Department of Insurance, "Sustainable Insurance Strategy," https://www.insurance.ca.gov/01-consumers/180-climate-change/Sustainable-Insurance-Strategy-Updates.cfm, accessed May 31, 2025.

65 Steven Greenhut, "State insurance crisis: Ricardo Lara emerges as an unsung hero," *The Orange County Register,* March 31, 2025, https://www.ocregister.com/2025/03/21/state-insurance-crisis-ricardo-lara-emerges-as-an-unsung-hero/

66 Ibid.

67 Krysten Crawford, "Who's paying the price for California's wildfires? 'Everyone.'," Stanford Institute for Economic Policy Research (SIEPR), https://siepr.stanford.edu/news/whos-paying-price-californias-wildfires-everyone\

68 Office of Gov. Gavin Newsom, "Governor Newsom signs executive order to help Los Angeles rebuild faster and stronger," www.gov.ca.gov/2025/01/12/governor-newsom-signs-executive-order-to-help-los-angeles-rebuild-faster-and-stronger/

69 Ibid.

70 Ibid.

71 Rachel Becker, "A salty dispute: California Coastal Commission unanimously rejects desalination plant," *CalMatters,* May 12, 2022, https://calmatters.org/environment/2022/05/california-desalination-plant-coastal-commission/

72 Senate Bill 423, LegiScan, https://legiscan.com/CA/text/SB423/id/2845314

73 "About Senate Bills 9 and 10," City of San Jose, https://
    www.sanjoseca.gov/your-government/departments-offices/
    planning-building-code-enforcement/planning-division/city-
    wide-planning/opportunity-housing/about-senate-bills-9-10,
    accessed May 31, 2025.

74 Kerry, Jackson, "Smart LA is a not-so-bright way to rebuild
    Los Angeles," Free Cities Center, Feb. 7, 2025, https://www.
    pacificresearch.org/smartla-is-a-not-so-bright-way-to-rebuild-
    los-angeles/

75 Clement Lau, "Rebuilding Smarter: How LA County Is
    Guiding Fire-Ravaged Communities Toward Resilience,"
    Planetizen News, April 27, 2025, https://www.planetizen.com/
    news/2025/04/134858-rebuilding-smarter-how-la-coun-
    ty-guiding-fire-ravaged-communities-toward#:~:text=next%20
    25%20years.-,Rebuilding%20Smarter:%20How%20LA%20
    County%20Is%20Guiding%20Fire%2DRavaged%20Commu-
    nities,broader%20sustainability%20and%20climate%20goals.

76 Karrie Jacobs, "In the Aftermath: How Should Los Angeles
    Rebuild After the Fires?" *The Nation,* May 19, 2025, www.
    thenation.com/article/society/rebuilding-la-after-the-fires/

77 Ibid.

78 Andrew Hay and Brad Brooks, "After fires, Los Angeles gets
    moonshot moment to rebuild," Reuters, Jan. 30, 2025, https://
    www.reuters.com/world/us/after-fires-los-angeles-gets-moon-
    shot-moment-rebuild-2025-01-30/

79   Office of Mayor Karen Bass, "Mayor Bass Issues Sweeping Executive Order to Clear Way for Angelenos to Rebuild Their Homes Fast," Jan. 13, 2025, https://mayor.lacity.gov/news/mayor-bass-issues-sweeping-executive-order-clear-way-angelenos-rebuild-their-homes-fast

80   Ben Christopher, "Newsom picks more housing over CEQA in backing two bills meant to speed construction," *CalMatters,* May 14, 2025, https://calmatters.org/housing/2025/05/newsom-ceqa-yimby-housing/

81   Felicia Mello, "Private firefighters are increasingly popular with insurers. But do they pose a risk?" *CalMatters,* Jan. 17, 2025, https://calmatters.org/housing/2025/01/private-firefighters-insurers/

82   Kenneth Schrupp, "California bill would ban private firefighters from using hydrants, cites public good," *Center Square,* March 5, 2025, https://www.thecentersquare.com/california/article_0494b20e-f9e8-11ef-a8e5-6f0abed9cb10.html

83   Federal Emergency Management Administration, Registry of firefighters, https://apps.usfa.fema.gov/registry/summary

84   Felicia Mello, "Private firefighters are increasingly popular with insurers. But do they pose a risk?" *CalMatters,* Jan. 17, 2025, https://calmatters.org/housing/2025/01/private-firefighters-insurers/

85   Transparent California database, https://transparentcalifornia.com/

86 Kenneth Schrupp, "California bill would ban private firefighters from using hydrants, cites public good," March 5, 2025, *Center Square,* https://www.thecentersquare.com/california/article_0494b20e-f9e8-11ef-a8e5-6f0abed9cb10.html

87 Steven Greenhut, "Sadly, selling out to unions is key to GOP success," *The Orange County Register,* March 25, 2022, https://www.ocregister.com/2022/03/25/sadly-selling-out-to-unions-is-key-to-gop-success/

88 Laurel Wamsley, "Private firefighters are helping in California fires. Is it fair?" NPR, Jan. 18, 2025, www.npr.org/2025/01/18/nx-s1-5265301/california-wildfires-private-firefighters

89 County of San Diego, Planning & Development Services, Vegetation Clearing FAQ Sheet, www.sandiegocounty.gov/content/dam/sdc/pds/docs/pds800.pdf

90 Tahoe Donner Association website, https://www.tahoedonner.com/

91 Zoe Meyer, "Tahoe Donner Association signs landmark wildfire insurance policy tied to forest management," *Sierra Sun,* May 2, 2025, https://www.sierrasun.com/news/tahoe-donner-association-signs-landmark-wildfire-insurance-policy-tied-to-forest-management/

92 Office of Gov. Gavin Newsom, "Governor Newsom signs legislation investing additional $170 million to prevent catastrophic wildfires, issues executive order to fast-track projects," April 14, 2025, https://www.gov.ca.gov/2025/04/14/governor-newsom-signs-legislation-investing-additional-170-million-to-prevent-catastrophic-wildfires-issues-executive-order-to-fast-track-projects/

93   Sen. Mike McGuire, "State Senate Unveils Major Wildfire Package: 'The Golden State Commitment,' Investing in a More Fire-Safe California," Feb. 11, 2025, https://sd02.senate.ca.gov/news/state-senate-unveils-major-wildfire-package-golden-state-commitment-investing-more-fire-safe

94   Free Cities Center video interview with Melissa Caen, June 17, 2025, https://www.pacificresearch.org/watch-are-crime-and-homelessness-shifting-san-francisco-right/

95   Noah Smith, "Learn smart lessons from the L.A. fires, not stupid lessons." *Noahpinion Substack,* Jan. 9, 2025, https://www.noahpinion.blog/p/learn-smart-lessons-from-the-la-fires

About the Author

STEVEN GREENHUT is a longtime journalist who has covered California politics since 1998. He wrote this book for the San Francisco-based Pacific Research Institute, where he founded that think tank's Sacramento-based journalism center in 2009 and is director of its Free Cities Center. He currently is western region director for the R Street Institute, a Washington, D.C.-based free-market think tank, and is on the editorial board of the Southern California News Group. Greenhut has worked fulltime as a columnist for *The Orange County Register* and *The San Diego Union-Tribune*. He writes weekly for *American Spectator* and *Reason* magazines. He is the editor of the PRI book *Saving California*, and the author of *Winning the Water Wars, Abuse of Power* and *Plunder*. He is also the author of the Free Cities Center booklets *Back from Dystopia: A New Vision for Western Cities; Putting Customers First: Re-Envisioning our Approach to Transportation Planning; Giving Housing Supply a Boost: How to Improve Afford ability and Reduce Homelessness* (with Dr. Wayne Winegarden)*; Building Cities from Scratch: America's Long History of Urban Experimentation;* and *Is There a War on Suburbia? Calling a Truce in the Battle Over Land Use.*

About Pacific Research Institute

The Pacific Research Institute (PRI) champions freedom, opportunity, and personal responsibility by advancing free-market policy solutions. It provides practical solutions for the policy issues that impact the daily lives of all Americans, and demonstrates why the free market is more effective than the government at providing the important results we all seek: good schools, quality health care, a clean environment, and a robust economy.

Founded in 1979 and based in San Francisco, PRI is a non-profit, non-partisan organization supported by private contributions. Its activities include publications, public events, media commentary, community leadership, legislative testimony, and academic outreach.

Center for Business and Economics

PRI shows how the entrepreneurial spirit—the engine of economic growth and opportunity—is stifled by onerous taxes, regulations, and lawsuits. It advances policy reforms that promote a robust economy, consumer choice, and innovation.

Center for Education

PRI works to restore to all parents the basic right to choose the best educational opportunities for their children. Through research and grassroots outreach, PRI promotes parental choice in education, high academic standards, teacher quality, charter schools, and school-finance reform.

Center for the Environment

PRI reveals the dramatic and long-term trend toward a cleaner, healthier environment. It also examines and promotes the essential ingredients for abundant resources and environmental quality: property rights, markets, local action, and private initiative.

Center for Health Care

PRI demonstrates why a single-payer Canadian model would be detrimental to the health care of all Americans. It proposes market-based reforms that would improve affordability, access, quality, and consumer choice.

Center for California Reform

The Center for California Reform seeks to reinvigorate California's entrepreneurial self-reliant traditions. It champions solutions in education, business, and the environment that work to advance prosperity and opportunity for all the state's residents.

Center for Medical Economics and Innovation

The Center for Medical Economics and Innovation aims to educate policymakers, regulators, health care professionals, the media, and the public on the critical role that new technologies play in improving health and accelerating economic growth.

Free Cities Center

The Free Cities Center cultivates innovative ideas to improve our cities and urban life based around freedom and property rights – not government.